DESCRIPTION
BEGGARED

or

The Allegory of Whiteness

Mac Wellman

BROADWAY PLAY PUBLISHING INC
New York
www.broadwayplaypublishing.com
info@broadwayplaypublishing.com

First edition: June 2019
I S B N: 978-0-88145-766-7

Book design: Marie Donovan
Page make-up: Adobe InDesign
Typeface: Palatino

DESCRIPTION BEGGARED, originally titled
WHITENESS, was commissioned by the Actors Theatre
of Louisville, Mark Masterson, Artistic Director.

CHARACTERS & SETTING

UNCLE FRASER, *Fraser Outermost Ring, a damnable marplot*

AUNT BIANCA, *a sort of human Blank, perhaps a parrot*

COUSIN JULIA, *called "The Eraser" because of a wicked habit she has*

MOTH, *an elegant older person*

LOUISA, *something of a ninny (not really); she doubles as the* DISPUTANT, *who possesses*

two ASSISTANTS; *a* PHOTOGRAPHER, *and two* MUSICIANS.

The floor is circular, a Malevich white-on-white target; time noodles around the here and now, whatever that may be.

NOTE

The occasional appearance of an asterisk in the middle of a speech indicates that the next speech begins to overlap at that point. A double asterisk indicates that a subsequent speech (not the one immediately following begins to overlap) at that point. The overlapping speeches are all clearly marked in the text.

Unto a life which I call natural I would
gladly follow even a will-o-the-wisp
through bogs and sloughs unimaginable,
but no moon nor firefly has shown me
the causeway to it. Nature is a personality
so vast and universal that we have never
seen one of her features.
Thoreau, *Walking*

*(Scene [Steam]: A party in a hypothetical Newport, Rhode Island; late summer; only something has gone wrong, radically wrong, during the taking of the annual family photograph; present are The Marplot [*UNCLE FRASER*], AUNT BIANCA and COUSIN JULIA [the Eraser], MOTH and LOUISA, [the one they call The Ninny]; and two MUSICIANS. And a very frustrated PHOTOGRAPHER, standing next to an enormous silver-plate camera. Everyone is gossiping [at the same time] animatedly about everyone else; there is a lot of bad jazz. Abruptly the bad jazz stops.)*

THE PHOTOGRAPHER: *(In horror)*
Cousin Julia the Eraser.

HORN GIRL:
They don't call her The Grande Parade for nothing.

(Bad jazz starts up once more.)

JULIA: *(In a rage)*
Whited sepulchers. Whited hypocrites and
creatures of the blench. Blenched and two-
faced, the whole bloody lot.* We get
together once a blue moon, once a
decade, once a century, once a millennium,
and you see the incredible result. Chaos. A
horrid, nasty scene. A picture of the most
appalling kind. A model of indecorous
outrage and unhinged incivility. Injured
merit run amuck.
Observe the Marplot there. Fraser is so filled
with swarthy venom he must disrupt this, this
most innocent of occasions.

Can he hear me? No, of course not. Too
wrapped up in his own foul rancor, a
whirlwind of a man. A local disturbance
posing as one of us. A hypothetical
human.

BIANCA:
And I was doing nothing harmful; and I was
doing nothing of the kind; and I was merely
minding my own business when the two of
them, yes, the two of them swept down
upon me like the spider; yes, very much the
spider.
(She makes the spider.)
The two of them, with their eight legs
arranged just so. The two of them, yes
*(Creeping sideways in her idea of spidery motion, her long
red tongue lolling.)*

*(BIANCA stops; looks over her shoulder to see if FRASER is
noticing her; he is not; reprise.)*

BIANCA:
And* I was doing nothing harmful, etc.

FRASER:
Can you believe it?* I am surrounded by maniacs
and idiots. It is hard to say which is
worse, the maniacs or the idiots. It is hard
to say which is worse, the mania of the
maniacs, or the idiocy of the idiots. For if
there is one thing I cannot abide it is the
mania of maniacs; for if there is
something I hate even more than that it
is the idiocy of idiots.
And the worst…
(He rages silently.)
And the worst is the idiocy of bad jazz, and the
noise of these infernal idiots and maniacs, idiots

and maniacs as you see arrayed all about me. Me!
Arrayed all about in a way that I find… Arranged in
obsequious propinquity. Arranged in a way
cunningly contrived to inflict the maximal insult upon
the auditory person of my personhood.
(He dances a jig of insult. Reprise)

MOTH:
I am the only soft one; I am the only soft
one, even though I am not covered with
fur. Yes, not with fur. I am the only soft
one; I am the only soft one, because I
am covered with feathers. Yes, with
feathers. Not with fur.
Yes.
Yes. The others are not covered with feathers.
Yes. With fur, look at them. Fur.
Yes. And I should have stayed home.
Yes, I should have stayed, and rested
quietly behind the floral screen, in my very
own room.
Yes, behind the floral screen, where I love to sit in
the darkness reading the geometrical writings
of Isaac Ring Barlow, our ancestor. Yes and yes,
I should have stayed at home, behind the
floral screen, in my own little room, eating a
prickled bloatfish,
there,
in suburban Kama-Loka, where I grew up. Curious.
(She smiles and shows her good teeth.)

JULIA:
When we were young, we girls sang a song
about Fraser. I shall sing it now:
Curious
Curious is the man

Curious the man
who has time to fiddle
hack upon a can
but not to riddle
the heart of man, nor his piddle;
Curious the man
who has time to fiddle.
Curious

whether boy or girl;
whether top or swirling
curiosity.
O black black black
hearted curiosity.

(Reprise by all the women)

LOUISA:
Er,

(Poor MOTH *faints in horror.)*

LOUISA:
All this is my fault, I suppose, and, er…
It is true that I am a ninny though my name
is not that, er…
It is Louisa; but I am called "Ninny" because
as a child, I visited with some distant relatives,
strange white people from the deep, interior regions
of Rhode Island's vast wasteland
and was told many wondrous things, er…
well, I suppose it comes down to that:
I told my parents how…how impressed
I was by those strange people, not to
mention their whiteness which was of an extraordinary
kind;

(All stop to hear what LOUISA *is about to confess:)*

LOUISA:
and, well, I said to them, my parents, I mean,

er…
I want to be one of them when I grown up.

(All turn slowly to regard LOUISA *with cold condescension.)*

(Pause)

(All look away.)

LOUISA:
So, I guess, well, I guess you could say
I was a real big disappointment.

*(The Marplot breaks out of the freeze and begins a
confidential talk to some of the members of the audience.)*

FRASER:
Can you believe it? Can you? Well, I can't.
Because actually it is quite beyond whatever
we mean when we call something "unbelievable".
Such a pretty girl, and so stupid. Yes,
so profoundly stupid that her stupidity
possesses a pallor that is almost…
*(He considers the question of what might constitute an apt
comparison.)*
…that is almost godly; in other words,
a whiteness that simply beggars description.
And all this must be the outcome of some genetic
predisposition or some ancient curse laid upon
our tribe by…
(A glimmer of insight)
Who knows? By some other tribe of equally
ancient, but heathenish morons…
(A more substantial glimmer)
I am referring to those ancient and heathenish
ones who occupied the place even before us.
(A pause for reflection)
If indeed the place could be said to have been
occupied at that remote time, because it is clear

that in the absence of our occupation the place
can hardly be thought of as a place, place *qua* place.
A place actual, that is.
No, for in our absence a place cannot
be said to constitute a place, only an
emptiness.
A noplace.
A primeval wasteland, devoid…
*(He illustrates what it is he is attempting to convey with a
motion of hand and arm.)*
(Pause. He does this again, it was so much fun.)
(However;)
*(clearly such gestures are not The Marplot's long suit, and
so he gives it up.)*

*(Seeing him apparently conclude his remarks, the
MUSICIANS start up their machines again, and we hear more
Bad Jazz.)*

FRASER:
Stop…stop…stop* that hideous din.

JULIA:
Oh Fraser, do put a lid on it, will you?
(She steps forth, imperiously; a magnificent specimen.)

*(LOUISA in particular is impressed by JULIA's aristocratic
bearing:)*

LOUISA:
This is a cousin—not of the moron variety—
but of another, equally drastic: Cousin Julia,
Cousin Julia, called The Eraser because her visits
tend to be accompanied by an unexpected removal,
so that these visits are much feared by the rest
of the family; er,
Cousin Julia has just returned from a trip
to Jerusalem, where she has become a…a
jewel.

FRASER:
A monstrous carbuncle, one might say.

JULIA:
Just who am I? you ask and since you pose that
question I shall give you a fit reply. I am The
Grand Parade, and that is the whole of it. That
is also why I am universally feared and respected.
Yes, I am she who guarantees when
a way is found that it be the right way
because what good would a way possibly
be if it were not the correct way? The splendor
of my being shall illuminate all these matters
until the time comes.

LOUISA:
Er,

JULIA:
Please do not interrupt.
Yes, my dear, The Grand Parade must run,
run and run her course till what has been
implied has taken on manifestation, a local
habitation, and born the shame of such.

LOUISA:
No, I was merely going to point out, however,
weakly and without conviction, that it has
begun snowing. Even though it is still September.

(A pregnant pause, as it has indeed begun to snow.)

(We hear, very quietly, The Siegfried Idyll.)

*(Or is the music emanating from some far stranger,
metaphysical domain?)*

*(All are deeply concerned about this question, but none of
them wishes anyone else to be aware of his or her concern.)*

(An Aryan pause)

FRASER:
It *is* snowing, of course. What of it?

BIANCA:
May I go back to the cupboard now?

JULIA:
Yes, Lady Blank, you may go back to your damnable
cupboard. Only see that you behave.

BIANCA:
Only the tiniest peek, I promise.

JULIA:
Only the tiniest.

(Scene begins to fade out strangely.)

MOTH:
And so, at the turn of the century, we all
assembled in this place, to greet the new
century, and yes, the new millennium, yes,
only somehow we got it dreadfully wrong.

JULIA: Radically wrong, one might say.
Drastically wrong.

(The Marplot turns away from them.)

(All turn to him.)

(An accusatory silence)

(From depths of his remoteness:)

FRASER:
Yes, yes. I know what you are thinking.
You are thinking it is Uncle Fraser's fault.
It is a problem I have with the black art, yes,
the black art of photography. And that problem
revolves with a regular orbicularity about an
unassailable truth: namely, that the
photographer's devilish craft involves the
complete effacement and wiping out of the
human soul. This process can be gradual

or instantaneous, depending on the relative
thickness or thinness of the spiritual entity
in question.

(FRASER *casts a significant glance at* The Ninny, *who looks
down abashedly.*)

FRASER:
I of course have suspected this all my life,
but did not arrive at a finished conclusion
until I had secured my fortune, and by implication
the fortune of the entire clan, with that old
enterprise in the depths...of the depths of the
Telegu Archipelago.

(All the women do something strange.)

FRASER:
Yes, yes. You scoff at things foreign. Strange
gods and the like. But after we signed
documents with the presiding fugleman in
Frontenac Bay, all went according to our
whitened way.

(A pale-faced pause)
Deep, deep truths I learned from my hetman
there, Baga and his catchild, Squeech. Deep,
deep things.

(A strange, slow and dark music breaks out.)

FRASER:
At the rituals we...we participated in,
as full equals, I might add....
(As Baga:)
WHATAMDISFER? WHATAMDEMFER?
WHATEMDOSFER? WHATAMYAMFER?
Or, more correctly:
WHAT AM DIS FOR? Holy holy holy.
WHAT AM DEM FOR? Lordy lordy lordy.

WHAT AM DOS FOR? Allalu, allalu, allalu.
WHAT AM YAM FOR? Blory, blory, blory.

(The MUSICIANS *take up the chant, quietly.)*

FRASER:
And, thus, even among the indigenous dwellers
of that remote region, the central questions revolve
just as they do for us; with, one might say, as
equal and perfect an orbicularity: Who am I?
What am I here for? Who are they? What are they
here for?

(Music ends.)

FRASER:
Baga and his catchild, Squeech. These were the first
to clarify the matter for me; the whiting out of the
oft photographed human soul.

JULIA:
All this feels rather arcane and superfluous, Fraser,
given the difficulty of assembling the family. All
at one time. All at any one place, that is.

FRASER:
I am resolved in my decision.

JULIA:
You have marred the occasion.

FRASER:
The occasion be damned.

(The PHOTOGRAPHER, *who has been standing idly by, rages
and chews on the brim of his hat.)*

JULIA:
The camera is prepared; the photographer has been
standing idly by; we shall be forced to proceed
without you.

FRASER:
I, the photographer be damned.

LOUISA:
Er,

(Another white pause)

(BIANCA abruptly sits down.)

(JULIA signals to the MUSICIANS.)

JULIA:
Aunt Blank, will you lead us in a few verses of the originary document?

(BIANCA brightens, gets up.)

BIANCA:
The family hymn?

JULIA:
Yes, my dear. That will do. After all, it is Founder's Day
and Founder's Day it shall be all day long, despite the black mood of Kaiser Fraser here.

(The MUSICIANS do their best as BIANCA begins, uncertainly:)

BIANCA:
Mine eyes have seen the something
of the coming of the Lord; he is
something something something
with his terrible swift sword…

(The song dissipates as it becomes apparent that neither BIANCA nor the MUSICIANS know what they are doing.)

(The scene piffles out.)

(All leave except The Marplot and The Ninny.)

FRASER:
Have they all gone?

LOUISA:
Not quite.

(And in fact: JULIA *and* BIANCA *are intently observing from just offstage, in the audience.)*

(Elsewhere, MOTH *observes both the observers and observed, herself unseen.)*

FRASER:
They have ruined me, Louisa, with their wicked
wicked obsession with establishing a visual
record of all events, even the most seeming innocent.

LOUISA: I don't know what to say.

—

BIANCA:
What are they saying?

JULIA:
How can I hear if you're always yapping?

BIANCA:
I think* they are talking about how you
turned Mother into an insect by an act of partial
erasure.

—

FRASER:
Well, they know what to say, Louisa. And
what they are saying they are saying
about you and me; some of it about you and
the greater part no doubt about me, and
all of it revolting.

LOUISA:
They mean well enough, Uncle Fraser.
They can't help being who they are, vague
and insubstantial. Fraught with the intangible.
These qualities go with the terrain of their
awful whiteness.

—

MOTH:
I think all of this is very silly. I think
all of this is so very silly, so silly I am going to
tell you all a little story about the olden days
when the vast metropolis of Newport had
not been dreamt of. Long before our
ancestors had discovered the principle,
long hidden, of certain, wonderful flea circuses
far away in the Telegu Islands, and came
shortly thereafter to corner the market
here. Long before Fraser, who was just a
young boy (I think it was this Fraser),
who had not yet developed such a malign and
flinty dislike of all things associated
with mechanical flea circuses and other
miniature, wind-up automata. A profound
hatred of all miniatures, be they natural,
or artificial.
Long before Grandfather Lockhart
stood up during a performance of the
Ninth Symphony at the Crystal Pavilion
and took the bullet meant for Governor
Gormley, a big, bald, whitish sort of man,
and was declared a hero in his abrupt
deconstruction.

—

LOUISA:
She's talking about imaginary things again,
Uncle Fraser. Decompression. Shadow
dances on the Neman River in old
Byelorussia. White Russia. Lovemaking
under a pontoon bridge on Decoration Day.

FRASER:
She has changed into one of them.

LOUISA:
What?

FRASER:
A lepidopteran.

MOTH:
Long before that, indeed. Long before Cousin Julia
the Eraser erased the last two letters from
my good maternal appelative and spat them out
at poor little infant Louisa Outermost...

LOUISA:
Er,

FRASER:
What is it?

LOUISA:
Er. I said "Er".

FRASER:
Be quiet then.

LOUISA:
It has started to snow again.

MOTH:
And long before my own Great Uncle, Tom Blank,
exhibited his device at the World's Fair
in Providence, the Rhode Island White-tailed
Dioptrical Silver Plate, in whose shimmer
shimmer even the Negro and his Negress might take
in the radiant whiteness of his and her eternal
Christian soul.

—

JULIA:
What are they talking about now?

BIANCA:
Something about going to the cemetery.

Putting up a monument to the Bishop
He wrote books, I think.

JULIA:
Who wrote books?

BIANCA:
The Bishop. He collected things too. They tell me
he was a bug man.

JULIA:
What?

BIANCA:
He had these pieces of cork with needles in
them, and he catches bugs and sticks them
on. We don't understand these things but
it's true, just the same. Can I go to the kitchen
and look at the Chiffonnier?

———

(Something strange happens.)

(All stop whatever they are doing; and)

*(missing a beat, try to figure out, privately, what has gone
awry; they attempt to do this without being detected.)*

JULIA:
What did you say?

BIANCA:
I forget, something about wanting to go
back to the kitchen.

JULIA:
And just what would you be up to, if
you should do that?

BIANCA:
Well…ah…

JULIA
Yes.

BIANCA:
Well, since Lady Moth seems to be preoccupied
with a fit of fantastical reminiscence, I shall
maybe, at any rate, I might…ah…

JULIA:
Yes. I think I know.

BIANCA:
If you think you know, why do you ask me?

JULIA:
I am hoping, dear Bianca, that I have
misjudged your intentions.

BIANCA:
Well, I thought with all these temporarious
disturbances, what with everyone acting
like the white mouse trapped within the
tikum-tokum of an originary Diophantine
Challenge Box…
The original model came only in alabaster
and Mother of Pearl. Even the
brilliant porches of Newport were not so
brilliant, but…dear me…I have quite
lost the thread of my idea.

JULIA:
That is because you are being evasive.

BIANCA:
Was I really?

JULIA:
Yes you were.

BIANCA:
Funny, I was not aware of being evasive.

JULIA:
That is not a justification.

BIANCA:
Do you think my lost thread of thought
requires a justification?

JULIA: There is a justification, or the implication
of one floating about in the fluid suspension
of your consciousness, my dear. Just asking
to be rubbed out.

BIANCA:
| My word, Julia. You make it sound like
we are bobbing for apples.

JULIA: —

BIANCA: —

—

(The MUSICIANS *mutter in their corner, their hushed voices,
strange, barely human. They sound like rodents.)*

MUSICIAN ONE:
They call him The Marplot because he's a grump.

MUSICIAN TWO:
They call him something like that, I suppose.

MUSICIAN ONE:
He hates us. He hates the music we make.

MUSICIAN TWO:
He is rich. And large, and white. He can get angry
at whomever he will.

MUSICIAN ONE:
He hates us because he is one of us.

MUSICIAN TWO:
You don't say? Say, he and that ninny niece
of his are making faces at us.

(Indeed, they are. Quite ugly faces)

MUSICIAN ONE:
He is a hateful grump. And a grouch.

MUSICIAN TWO:
What is a grouch?

MUSICIAN ONE:
Similar to the grump, but worse.
Worse as rat is to mouse.

MUSICIAN TWO:
Worse.

MUSICIAN ONE:
Yes, much worse.
(Ruminative pause. He scratches his hump [he has a hump].)
Then why have we been hired to play music here?

MUSICIAN TWO:
His wicked cousin, the one they call The
Grand Parade has arranged the whole business.
My surmise is that, in a previous life, he
was an inventor of music boxes and mechanical
flea circuses himself*...but I cannot be
entirely sure...

FRASER:
What are you saying, my good man? What
idiotic calumny are you giving voice to?
You have laid siege to my wits with
this expensive, idiotic noise.

JULIA:
Music, it is called, Fraser. Please desist from this
outrageous behavior. They are only doing as they have
been commissioned.

FRASER:
Noise, noise, noise.

(The MUSICIANS *start up in a fury.)*

*(*FRASER *dances his angry jig.)*

FRASER: Expensive noise then.
A stench in the ear.

(The two MUSICIANS *sing:)*

MUSICIANS:
Description is the beggar
rolling up the floor
cutting up the carpet
upon which the Devil poured
bleach of his depiction,
whirling like a djinn,
pure description beggared
White as sin.

White as sin; white as sin;
white as description beggared
whirling like a djinn
whirling like a djinn.
White as sin; white as sin.

—

*(Reprise. All begin to whirl, their white clothes like
monstrous blooms rotating around them.)*

(They sing:)

MUSICIANS:
In the white squall
of the metaphysical ocean.
Ocean, ocean, ocean.

White as sin; white as sin;
white as description beggared.
Whirling like a djinn.
White as sin
White as sin

—

(Music stops suddenly—as a mean and petty practical
joke of the two MUSICIANS. They hide a cackle.

(All the others look somewhat embarrassed.)

(In this awkward moment, MOTH *chooses to start up her*
story again:)

MOTH:
...and long before that; and long before that even,
and before the time we celebrate on Founder's Day
and before, yes, even before the signing of the
originary document and the preliminary description;
and before even the first voyage of our brave
ancestor to the Isthmus of Telegu...and the
station at Whydah, along the bleached, bone-white
sands of Dahomey;
and before the invention of the Rhode Island
Silver Plate Dioptrical Flea Circus, and all
the various types of music box:
those of ivory and those of horn;
those of the right, and those of the left brain;
those of the angel who is the wandering
    albatross, and those of the imp Obsidian
    whose weight forces the fulcrum up,
    whose weight forces the fulcrum down;
and before even the naming of names;
of Leucoblast and Leucorrhea;
of Leucocyte and Leucocytosis;
of Leucoderma and Saint Leukemia;
of all things so turned and so leprous
    they outwhite oblivion; for

(Softly; all the women join in the song, as this is a ritual
from the olden days; all conventional lights dim; but black
light comes in.)

MOTH & WOMEN:
In every town, there is a white girl;
whiter than the rest, whiter
than snow, whiter
than corn tassel, whiter than

wheat flowing in the evening breeze;
whiter than the air we breathe;
(*A fluffy white silencio*)

Whiteness is the color of what
want is. Whiteness is want;
what we all want, not knowing.

(*A choral reprise*)
In every town, there is a white girl
whiter than
the rest;
whiter than the air we breathe;
breathe.

MOTH: (*Once more*)
And I thought I was that girl.* I was, I confess,
that girl.

FRASER:
I should have stayed at home, Louisa.

LOUISA:
Oh, Uncle Fraser, cool it, will you?
Dear Moth is entitled to her imaginary
raptures.

FRASER:
All this resembles nothing so much
as a Sikkimese hangover.

JULIA:
Don't like it, Fraser, when the hens come
home to roost?

FRASER:
Witchetty, all of it. Witchetty. Witchetty.
Witchetty.

LOUISA:
What's "Witchetty"?

JULIA:
What in the name of Great Aunty Dahlia
do you mean?

(Aunt BIANCA *brightens.)*

(A music of ominous footfalls.)

(A transcendental music lifts our souls.)

(Pause)

BIANCA:
I was just getting around to that.

LOUISA:
"Witchetty". What's it mean?

FRASER:
How the devil should I know?

(A strange, little man enters. This is the WHITE DWARF. *All freeze except The Marplot, who is the only one to see him.)*

(The WHITE DWARF, *like the others, is dressed entirely in white except for a red fez with a black tassel.)*

(This is the only scenic color in the play [well, almost].)

(The WHITE DWARF *mutters to himself angrily. We do not hear much of what he says.)*

———

(He limps over to an audience member [a shill]; grabs that person's program; bites it and growls; rips the program into pieces; stomps on the pieces, and rolls around on the stage scratching at them with his hind feet, rather like a nasty housecat with her prey.)

(The Marplot watches all this in horror.)

(A Dwarfish pause)

(Suddenly the WHITE DWARF *catches sight of the Marplot, gets to his feet, and begins to mutter again. We hear only the following amidst his demented garble and cackling.)*

THE WHITE DWARF:
"Witchetty"! Witchetty, ha. It's all one big Polo
Bear bottom. One big white torpedo. An obsessional
white horde, ha!
(Now he begins taking flash pictures of FRASER *with his
instant Kodak.)*

(The latter grimaces in the agony of unwilling exposure;)

(but the WHITE DWARF *continues, briefly, examining each
photo before discarding it with gleeful contempt;)*

(The WHITE DWARF *moons The Marplot, who thereupon
faints.)*

*(Before exiting, he places his visiting card in The Marplot's
open mouth.)*

—

(A stuffed ZEBRA, *on wheels, appears just at the lip of
the stage. Greeting this with delight, the* WHITE DWARF
*carefully places his camera on the stage, where it shall
remain for the rest of the play, lit by a pin-light.)*

(Pause)

(The transcendental music stills.)

(The WHITE DWARF *hobbles off, with the zebra [his trophy]
in tow.)*

(The MUSICIANS *are the first to snap out of it, and begin to
play in a more soothing vein—but still their old Bad Jazz.)*

—

BIANCA:
I said. I was just getting around to that.

JULIA:
Getting around to what?

*(The Ninny spies The Marplot stretched out at her feet, and
let's out a short but energetic scream.)*

(Lights back to normal)

(All focus on him; MOTH alone smiles because, with all her years and wisdom, she finds the scene amusing;)

(LOUISA leans over to remove from FRASER's open mouth the visiting card which the WHITE DWARF has placed there. She reads:)

LOUISA:
Parking lot of the Wallmart on Route 7.
Near the dumpster. At the back of the
abandoned Weiss Mechanical-Musical Flea
Circus Factory. This Tuesday. Four P M.
Be there. The Dwarf will lead you on
from there. White Whiskey John, Assistant
to the Disputant.

(The Marplot has come to his senses, but is still groggy;)

(turns to MOTH, almost tearful.)

JULIA:
Disputant? We shall have no disputes
during the holiday. Fraser, what does
this mean?

LOUISA:
I'm sure there is a rational explanation,
cousin Julia.

BIANCA:
Moth, what can this mean? Whatever can this
mean?

LOUISA: White whiskey John?

MOTH: It's a kind of shrike.

(All look at MOTH with surprise.)

BIANCA:
And what I was going to suggest is that we
call it a day, since the photographer seems
to have disappeared.

(All look at JULIA, *who feigns innocence.)*

BIANCA:
And Fraser has suffered from a stroke or other
moral lapse;
and the musicians, or whatever they are,
have assumed a dark and gloomy aspect,
probably because they are waiting to be
paid; and they shall not be paid;
And they shall not be paid
   because there is no money to pay them with;

(The music stops.)

BIANCA:
And they shall not be paid,
   because they are dark and witchetty, and
   possibly in league with the Adversary;
And they shall not be paid,
   because given the family structure, it is
   unclear who among us holds the authority
   and controls the purse-strings governing
   the writing of checks;
And they shall not be paid,
   because their music is of a disturbing kind,
   and lacks the melodious harmoniousness which
   above all the family fancies on these occasions,
   such as Founder's Day, or the Day of the Signing
   of the Originary Document; or on
White-Handed Goose Day; or
Woonsocket Day; or
Gravity Feed Day; or
Moon Dead Dog Day; or
Anna Innermost Ring Day; or
on Prickled Bloatfish Day...or...

JULIA:
You are not making any sense, Bianca.

BIANCA:
That is because I wish to return to my little room,
and hide behind my little floral screen…

JULIA:
We all wish to return to our little rooms, and we
all wish to hide behind our little floral screens,
but all the rest of us have the internal fortitude
and the will power to resist that temptation.

BIANCA:
I know, I know, I know.

(Pause. Something happens in the vicinity of The Marplot's nose.)

(Something connected to the idea of butterflies.)

(Suddenly FRASER sits bolt upright. Perhaps he is aware of the possibility of the WHITE DWARF's return.)

JULIA:
In fact, Bianca. In fact you are resorting
to your old bad habits.

BIANCA:
Julia, how can you say that? In what way
can I be said to be resorting to my old
bad habits?

JULIA:
You know.

BIANCA:
I do not know.

JULIA:
Yes you do.

BIANCA:
No I don't.

(A standoffish pause)

JULIA:
Yes you do.

BIANCA:
No I don't,

JULIA:
You know.

BIANCA:
I do not.

LOUISA:
Er,

JULIA:
Shut up, you feeble-minded white-handed tree-mouse.

BIANCA:
Just because I would like to tip-toe into the kitchen
and out the back way...

JULIA:
Yes?

BIANCA: Out the back way, and down the steps that
lead to the other place;

(Universal fear at the mere mention)

BIANCA:
The other place, you call the Gaming Room (FRASER);
and you (LOUISA)
call the Montessori Bughouse Underfloor Area;
and you (MOTH)
call the Highborn Muskrat Hideaway;
and you (MUSICIANS)
call the Take-After Take-Out Taj Majal;
and you, Julia, call the White-Haired White Leather
White Tie;
but is, in fact, only the antique cupboard,
or chiffonnier, that was Great Aunt Dahlia's.

JULIA:
And is now her final resting place.

BIANCA:
I only want a teensy peek. Teensiest of the
teensy.

JULIA:
It is a low, depraved wish on your
part, Bianca. Ancestor worship must
aspire to more elegant expression in our
contemporary Rhode Island, dear.

LOUISA:
Er,

JULIA:
Shut up, you hideous white crappie.

(*Shock*)

(*The Grand Parade gestures to the* MUSICIANS, *who begin to
play more or less morally affirming music—*)

JULIA:
Whited sepulchers. Whited hypocrites and…
and creatures of the blench. Blenched and…
two-faced, the whole bloody lot. Great Aunt
Dahlia has entered into the phase of her
long and rich existence we denominate
as her Egyptian Alabaster years; not
quite among the living; not quite among
the dead. So;
Bianca,
when we disturb her profound meditation
upon the higher things, transubstantiation and
the transmigration of the human soul, we
threaten her delicate equipoise. For good reason
she has returned to the enameled sanctuary of
her treasured chiffonnier, most treasured of all
the family heirlooms we possess;
Before her it belonged to Lydia Lockhart; and
before her to Anastasia, perhaps better known

as the natural daughter of Mr French Church;
and before that to Gloria Defiance Ring; and
before that to Philippa Outermost Ring; and
before that to Augusta Outermost Ring; and
in the beginning, before the signing of the originary
document, and before the framing of the preliminary
question, and the opening of the field and the
closing of the old Weiss factory across Route 7
and before the establishment of Founder's Day
which is also known in the local parlance
as Prickled Bloatfish Day; and before the
framing of the other question, the eternal one…
(In a whisper)
The one we dare not think too much about…
(A thoughtful pause)
…to Louisa Outermost Ring, for whom our
     silly little Louisa was named, named
     with the misguided hope that names truly
     are fates, as the philosopher Pseudo-Mennipus
     opined, and are not mere slank apellatives.

LOUISA:
But I thought she was dead.

JULIA:
She will be dead, silly, if Bianca continues to
disrupt her dream time flat line.

BIANCA:
So I am to have nothing for my trouble?

JULIA:
What trouble is that, Bianca?

BIANCA:
The trouble of driving here, all the way from my
little room in suburban Kama-Loka.

JULIA:
That is not such a far place. I drove all the
way from Paris, France.

MOTH:
Disaster, disaster, disaster.

JULIA: —

BIANCA: —

LOUISA:
Er,

JULIA:
Be quiet please.

LOUISA:
Er,

JULIA:
Please.

LOUISA:
Er, I was only going to point out that it has
begun to stop snowing.

(*All look about, as if to confirm or contradict this assertion.*)

JULIA:
It has begun to do no such thing.

(*Indeed, The Grand Parade is, on this occasion, quite
correct.*)

MOTH:
Disaster, disaster, disaster.

(*Aunt* BIANCA *lies down on the stage, and thrashes both
hands and feet in total postverbal frustration.*)

(*One of the* MUSICIANS *grows bold [the First].*)

(*All glare at him disapprovingly; he loses his nerve.*)

(BIANCA *rages once more.* MUSICIAN ONE's *nerve returns;
he approaches very close to* JULIA's *chin.*)

MUSICIAN ONE:
We will be paid.

JULIA:
I beg your pardon?

MUSICIAN ONE:
We have played some music, some pretty
darn good music and we will be* paid.

MUSICIAN TWO:
Yes. It is only right that, as god fearing
tax payers, that we be paid.

JULIA:
Go whistle for it then.

(All turn their backs on the poor MUSICIANS;)

(save MOTH *who has put on her snow shoes and trudged
out; and* FRASER *who is studying the card lately placed in
his mouth by The* WHITE DWARF.)

(Ambivalent as ever, LOUISA *does not know what to do, nor
with whom to sympathize so she counts imaginary rabbits as
they hop on her knee.)*

(After a stingy pause, MUSICIAN ONE *signals to* MUSICIAN
TWO *who thereupon sings a song:)*

MUSICIAN TWO:
I am in an economic hell;
bell, do not ring for me
bell, do not ring for me
bell, do not ring for me

because I am not...not at all
and I have lost my whiteness.

MUSICIAN ONE & TWO:
Have lost thereby,
lost my rightness, it's true.
And have lost my rightness.

MUSICIAN ONE, TWO & LOUISA:
Oh what a hell. Oh what a hell.

Oh, rabbit of loss
I am in an economic hell
Bell
tell me what to do.

(Humiliated, The Grand Parade opens her ratty little clutch purse, produces a coin; bites it; regrets biting as the taste is foul;)

(pauses;)

(and tosses the coin over her shoulder; the MUSICIANS *let the coin fall where it may; pause;)*

(then MUSICIAN ONE *signals* MUSICIAN TWO *who recovers the coin and pockets it.)*

—

*(*BIANCA *and* JULIA *slip out as* MUSICIAN ONE *signals once more to* MUSICIAN TWO *who begins to sing:)*

MUSICIAN TWO:
Beautiful girl, you are so fair*…

(The Marplot angrily and quite suddenly interjects:)

FRASER:
And just what the hell am I supposed to do
about this idiotic invitation?

LOUISA:
Er, I suppose you might want to take
the bull by the Melanesian antlers,
 | cross the road, as the message indicates
and see what lies on the other side.

*(*FRASER *considers this option; reconsiders.)*

FRASER:
Storm's approaching white out.

LOUISA:
Then you'd best stay at home.

FRASER:
Stay at home is what I should have
done in the first place, Louisa.
*(Dresses for the storm and vanishes into the storm like the
white-tailed deer.)*

(No one knows what to do for a second.)

*(LOUISA smiles fetchingly at the MUSICIANS who smile
back.)*

(MUSICIAN TWO begins to sing once more:)

MUSICIAN TWO:
Beautiful girl, you are so fair
I am made deaf;
one bite of your blanch
collides with my habit
and I shall fall down like the
moon.

ALL:
And I shall fall down like the
moon.
Blond beyond belief, and
wrecked upon the coco reef
of disbelief;
   belief in whiteness
   ultimate whiteness.
Whiteness alchemical;
whiteness metaphysical;
whiteness allegorical.
Beautiful girl, etc.

———

(Lights dim as the storm whitens.)

*(We catch sight of The Marplot trudging along in the
direction of the highway, and the abandoned Musical-
Mechanical Flea Circus Factory where his fateful
appointment is shortly to occur.)*

FRASER:
Witchetty. All of it, witchetty. What a hell
of a local disturbance is mankind…

(We see MOTH high up in a dormer window.)

MOTH:
Disaster, disaster, disaster.

*(The First Scene peters outs like the last of the white sand in
the hourglass.)*

*(First Entr'acte [Sleet]: The Marplot staggers through the
storm, as if on a treadmill. He passes the ghostly white
mansions of Astors and Vanderbilts; he mutters to himself.
Far above, on the metaphysical plane and surrounded by
fluffy white clouds are JULIA, BIANCA, LOUISA and MOTH;
they look down on FRASER's progress with transcendental
benignity—and softly sing, as before:)*

JULIA, BIANCA, LOUISA & MOTH:
Mine eyes have seen the something
of the coming of the Lord;
he is something something something
with his terrible swift sword.

FRASER:
Damn that crowd at the white horse tavern…
Damnable flea circuses.
God Damned Wanton-Lyman-Hazard House.
Witchetty. All of it vile and witchetty.
Damnable Samuel Whitehorse Museum.
Astors and Vanderbilts be damned, the whole
lot. Arrivistes and social climbers, all of 'em.

Isaac Bell? Phooh? I knew Isaac Bell
When he was shucking shellfish at a
third rate clam-shack down by the pier.
Damnable music-boxes. Witchetty and
damnable, the whole shebang.

(All fades to white.)

*(Scene [Snowy]: The vast interior of the abandoned factory.
Eerie light from a skylight high above. A very very long
table with a chair at each end. At the far end of this is The
DISPUTANT, cloaked in silvery whiteness [though shadowy]
and barely visible. Two ASSISTANTS hover nearby and
whisper in the DISPUTANT's ear. Light silvery laughter rises
from time to time, barely audible and barely human. The
Marplot enters and stands near the empty chair; he can only
just make out the distant figure for all the gloom. A silvery
pause)*

FRASER:
And so?

DISPUTANT:
Your name is Fraser Outermost Ring?

FRASER:
And so? What of it?

DISPUTANT:
Answer the question.

FRASER:
What question was that?

DISPUTANT:
Must I repeat myself, Mister Ring?

FRASER:
Why have I been summoned to this place?

DISPUTANT:
You are the fourth Ring to bear the family
name of Ring?

FRASER:
Why should I discuss my family name with you?

DISPUTANT:
And so? I might just as well reply, "And so?",
and then that leads us, in perfect circularity,
back to the beginning.

(A circular pause)

FRASER:
And so? What of it? What do you want from me?

DISPUTANT:
Maybe the whole point is that there is no issue
to any of it.

FRASER:
There is no point to any of WHAT? What the hell
are you driving at?

*(The distant figures consult and whisper. Light, silvery
laughter.)*

*(FRASER takes off his coat and drapes it carefully over the
back of the chair.)*

(He scratches his head.)

(He sits down upon the chair.)

DISPUTANT:
Why do you think you have been summoned here?

FRASER:
Have I been summoned here? I believe I came |
of my own free will.

DISPUTANT:
Do you imagine you are whiter than the rest?

FRASER:
Of course I am whiter than the rest.
All the Outermost Rings are whiter

than the rest. What the devil does that
have to do with the price of tea in Telegu?

(Silvery laugh)

DISPUTANT:
Quite the wit.

FRASER:
Runs in the family, on my mother's side at least.

DISPUTANT:
Quite the wit. Wit. From *Witan* in Old English:
to know. Are you the knower, Mister Fraser
Outermost Ring?

FRASER:
I misspoke: Wit does not run in the family.
Rather it runs from the family—idiots and
maniacs the whole bloody lot.

DISPUTANT:
Strawberry.

FRASER:
What? *(Clearly shaken)*

DISPUTANT:
Was that not the name?

FRASER:
I have no idea what you're talking about?

DISPUTANT:
Strawberry. As in strawberry blond—your nickname
as a youth in the remote, wild outer reaches of North
West Rhode Island some three thousand miles away,
where you and your young accomplices made balls out
of
the blubber of the white seal and toyed with the
bleached
skull of the Telegu white stork.

FRASER:
And so? What is the point of this?
Well, what if I did? What of it?

(A silvery pause)

DISPUTANT:
Is there not hell to pay? Hell, Fraser, hell?

CHORUS OF FIGURES:
>   Shake shake shake
>   Shake the devil off
>   in the name of Jesus.* *(X 7)*
And did you not play Taji in the school play;
Taji, lost in the mindless pursuit of Yillah?
Lovely, yellowhaired Yillah, she who was
whiter than the rest?

FRASER:
The part was a minor one.

DISPUTANT:
Cloud you speak closer to the machine,
Strawberry?

FRASER:
The part was a minor one. The play of no
significance. I have forgotten the whole matter
till this very moment.

DISPUTANT:
Your various selves seem to have a way
of sliding away from the central axis.

FRASER:
That is natural, is it not? I see nothing
wrong with that.

DISPUTANT:
Others in the family call you The Marplot
because you have a way of spoiling their
plans, Strawberry.

FRASER:
Their plans are often silly, silly ones. Plans
deserving of spoliation. And who in the name of Roger
Williams are you?

DISPUTANT:
I am your Disputant.

FRASER:
My what?* What is the name of hell is that?

DISPUTANT:
You heard me, Strawberry. I am your Disputant,
and you have been summoned to this place
to answer for some actions undertaken in
your name, by you and your other selves
and selflings—as the Millennium draws
nigh.

(The Marplot laughs.)

DISPUTANT:
In particular, you are accused of disrupting
the fundamental plan;
as proposed in the Originary Document;
as a response to the Preliminary Question, and
the opening of the field, and other cognate
selves and selflings relative to that question.

(FRASER *is stunned.)*

DISPUTANT:
In fact the whole family of Ring is responsible;
is responsible for these actions; actions which
have over the course of time beggared description,
and which have caused the heavenly dome of whitest
heaven
to be

(The DISPUTANT *and her* ASSISTANTS,)

(each & every one,)

(make a motion,)

(ever so slightly, of the hand.)

DISPUTANT:
To become smutched, to become as smutched
as the black orchid Taji brought to Yillah
in that high school play, foolishly thinking
that by so doing he would win her love.
Black as the teeth of the inhabitants of
Tsalal.

(FRASER reaches the boiling point.)

FRASER:
What does this have to do with me? I have
always been an exception to the white rule
of the Ring family.

DISPUTANT:
You are one of the central rings; the last, in fact,
of a long succession of Rings; you are, therefore,
a critical link in that deplorable argument.

FRASER:
And precisely what argument would that be?

DISPUTANT:
Enough of this backpeddling. You know
perfectly well what I am talking about.

FRASER:
Damnation. I had nothing whatsoever to do
with the evils you have alluded to. The
lunacy of the Ring family has nothing to do
with me. Why hound me? It is senseless.
Why not pursue your savage vendetta
against all the others? Cousin Julia, for
instance, the one they call The Eraser;
the one who calls herself The Grand Parade?
Cousin Julia the Eraser so called because
of her strange ability to cause people and

things to vanish. Whole epochs of the family
chronicle caused to disappear under the insidious
rub a dub dub of her India rubber eraser.
Most of the chronicle from the time of Fraser$_1$
and Fraser$_2$ reduced to powder, mere pulverized
rubber. Similarly, my own childhood, the time
of my own father, Fraser$_3$ has become, through her
doing, a horrid, white blank or blot. An empty page
in an old old book, once hallowed, now hollow.
Hollow through the vile praxis of Cousin Julia.

(The DISPUTANT *and her* ASSISTANTS *move about and make
a noise like crumpled paper.)*

FRASER:
Er, her visits are seldom. It is duly recorded:
Her visits are seldom, but much feared because
they are so terrible.
(Pensive. Grasping for straws)
Just now she has returned from a trip to
Jerusalem, where she has become a jewel.
Can you imagine?
As if we needed jewels after the vast fortune
I made lately in Durango, yes, in the uranium
mines at Durango; and somewhat earlier at
Telegu…
(His mind grows dim with hollow time.)
Yes, at the Isthmus of Telegu, where my
father's friend, Isidor—Isidor Weiss—
first devised the Weiss Semi-Pneumatic
Musical Flea Circus in…

DISPUTANT:
That was fifty-four years before your
birth, Fraser.

FRASER:
Well, what of it? *(Sputtering, confused)*

DISPUTANT:
You have confused your self with other
semi-erased fingers of your pseudogroup.
*(Holds up her hand, sheathed delicately in a white glove. She
moves her fingers ever so slightly.)*

FRASER:
What in the name of Babbalanja is that? A
pseudo-group?

DISPUTANT:
Identical selves—out of time they form a pure
group, white on white so to speak, of identical,
yet separate beings. I am speaking of Fraser the
first, Fraser the second, Fraser the third, and you:
Fraser the fourth. In it, time that is, they
fool eye and mind by an apparent difference that
both IS and is NOT the case.

(High above, near the skylight a white rag flutters.)

(All look up.)

(We hear the winter wind blow, blow whitely.)

(A dreadful pause)

FRASER:
Are you saying I am not who I am?

DISPUTANT:
In this particular instance, you have
confused your doing, the doing of
Fraser$_4$ with those of your ancestor,
Fraser$_1$.

(The Marplot is stunned.)

(He looks out: can this be?)

DISPUTANT:
You have confused Late Capitalism with
the dawn of the Wealth of Nations;
mediocrity with accomplishment;

parasitical decline with the miracle
of appearance.

(Sudden realization)

FRASER:
Oh, now I see.

(Quietly)
My own failings, modest though they be, are
to be confounded with those of my forebears.

DISPUTANT:
The others and selflings of your pseudogroup,
Strawberry.

(Light and silvery laughter)

FRASER:
I wish you would not use that...that turn
of phrase.

DISPUTANT:
And why not, Strawberry?

(FRASER lowers his head.)

FRASER:
It is just that it reminds me of so many
things I would just as soon forget.

DISPUTANT:
Like that clandestine meeting, with a certain
gentleman, at the Astor?

FRASER:
The encounter happened by chance, I swear.

DISPUTANT:
The bargain sworn on that day, or rather...
(With grim determination)
...late in the witching hours of that day,
did not happen by chance.

FRASER:
The version you recount is not the correct version.

DISPUTANT:
It is the version as recorded by you, in the
diary you kept for that year, and it is
in no way ambiguous. Your agreement
with that certain gentleman...
(A Whitish pause)
Specifies in great detail...

(ASSISTANTS snap their fingers seven times.)

(FRASER moves from one foot to the other.)

(He has forgotten, thus, that he is standing.)

DISPUTANT:
...the intended terms of the arrangement.

(The white rag in the skylight is ruffled, lightly—whitely.)

FRASER:
You have been speaking with Bianca, my
country cousin—the young ninny's aunt.

(Silence. Pause. Silence)

DISPUTANT:
Bianca, Bianca. Tsk, tsk.

(A hissing from the distant ASSISTANTS.)

DISPUTANT:
She was so, so pretty so long ago.
Her eyes the color of the deep ice we
sawed in massive cubes and hauled
up from White Wolf Lake.
All she is up to now is obsessional stuff.
Bianca wants to go to the kitchen, and to
the old cupboard or *chiffonnier*, which for
the good of all concerned has been closed to
public view these long years. She wants to
go to the kitchen so she may take a peek.

(He titters lightly and silvery, almost, but not quite)

(like the DISPUTANT's *two* ASSISTANTS.*)*

(This seems to make them uncomfortable.)

FRASER:
So she may take a peek (can you imagine?)

*(*BIANCA, MOTH, *and* JULIA *appear high above, in a floral cameo;)*

(they echo his last:)

BIANCA, MOTH, & JULIA:
…take a peek *(Can you imagine?)*

*(*FRASER *is a little unnerved by this.)*

FRASER:
Take a peek at Great Aunty Dahlia (whom
we call the Madwoman in the Cupboard)
whose exceptional pallor, you see, derives
from her complete innocence of the sun's
rays for seven full decades.
(He titters again, despite himself.)
Bianca we used to call Aunt Blank. You
might say she was totally erased by
Julia and became a radical. A lot of us
Rings were radicals in those days. But
then the bubble grew in swollen…in
swollen wonderment, and we all grew
richer even than the Rings who worked
for it. Yes, richer by far.
(He whistles in the bubble of his wonderment, intensely white.)
And so radical Aunt Blank went off to
gay Paree, much to the shame of the
family and became at first a photograph
(Can you imagine?); and then, and then:
and became a rhododendron;
and became a speck of hoarfrost;

and became a hangnail;
and became a doorstop;
and became a great white peach louse;
and became a whited sepulcher;
and BECAME A PARROT.

THE ASSISTANTS:
Shake shake shake
Shake shake shake
Shake shake shake
Shake the Devil off
in the name of Jesus.
Shake the devil off
in the name of Jesus. *(X 3)*

(FRASER acts as if he had done nothing unusual.)

DISPUTANT:
But we have strayed from the mark.

FRASER:
Indeed, we have. For the worst crime of all
also came about as a result of Julia's
penchant for the systematic removal of
all traces. For concealed within that penchant
lay the even deeper obsession, common to all
us Rings, Innermost and Outermost alike,
to go back to the starting point with a
series of…with a series of searching
questions.
And thus to initiate an interrogation,
in the simplest of language, but an
interrogation nevertheless. A drastic
interrogation.
Simple terms. Drastic interrogation.
Much like this one, in fact.

DISPUTANT:
And? And so?

FRASER:
And the long and short of it was that
Before Julia had quite gotten the hang
of it all (these two impulses being
in direct contradiction), she had
accidentally erased the last two
letters of her mother's good
name, and so transformed her from
A Mother into a Moth.

DISPUTANT:
And what did she do with the two letters
she had removed from her Mother's good
name?

FRASER:
Trick question. But I was prepared for it.
(He prepares himself further to reply; and replies:)
Thereupon she accidentally sneezed, and in
so doing accidentally obliterated poor
little Louisa's wits and replaced her
adolescent speech faculty with a single,
odd vocalization.

DISPUTANT:
And what was that vocalization?

FRASER:
Er,

(All three figures lean forward, as if mishearing.)

ALL THREE:
Beg your pardon?

FRASER:
Er. The letters E and R. Er. The fragments
of our own dear Moth's former matriarchal
appelative. Er.
(Amused by a peculiar thought)

At least we were able to keep the two
errant letters in the family.
(Suddenly sarcastic)
So that
We Outermost Rings are able, despite
all Bianca's slanders and Julia's
erasures, to perpetuate the miracle
of appearance, even amidst the sham
of the contemporary and likewise
the parasitical decline of our kind
in the debacle of Late Capitalism
you have so astutely alluded to.
The miracle of appearance and the
riddle of amazement. Yes, these
remain to our credit. White out!
Bull's-eye! White out!
(He gestures stiffly, but triumphantly;)
(just like Uncle Adolf in the railway car outside gay Paree.)

ALL THREE: *(Of his tormentors)*
Bull's eye! Ha!

(FRASER is caught offguard by this.)

DISPUTANT:
All this lies as far afield of the mark,

ALL THREE:
Strawberry;

DISPUTANT:
All of this lies as far afield of the mark
as the silver-tipped claw of the White Flaw
(Pausing for effect)
A kind of rooster you will* recall [Aw...

ASSISTANTS:
Aw…aw…aw… *(They flap arms as wings.)*

DISPUTANT:
…that was given to you, in the Ivory Room

of the Astor, by that certain gentleman,
oh, oh, oh, so long ago.
Do you recall that silver-tipped claw?

He is suddenly frightened by the snare.

FRASER:
That was not me. That was my great grandfather,
the primal Fraser, Kaiser Fraser, whose wicked ways
we in the family have long since amended;
amended, indeed and made up for, in various
noble ways...

DISPUTANT:
Made up for? How can what is fixed in
the past be so easily "made up" for?

FRASER:
Over the years we have given to the poor,
and mentally impaired; we have rewired the
chronically dislocated and restored the
oh so endangered...

ASSISTANTS:
And rare. And rare. And* rare.

FRASER:
endangered Sweet Ratfish to his
native habitat in the vast, oily
cypress bog region of Lower Rhode Island;
especially near Lake White Choler where
year round the mists hang heavy in
the spidery Spanish moss and sawgrass;

(Pause to see if his tack has taken; it has not.

FRASER:
established foundations and institutions for
the better class of Arts and Letters, those
tending toward the spiritual and moral correction
of the stained and blenched American soul;
I am referring to the Outermost Ring and

Plantation of Providence Foundation, and
her cousin at White Fin Harbor, The Prickled
Bloatfish Institute which is devoted to the,
ah,
reintroduction, ah,
(Clearly doesn't know what he is talking about.)
…of all that glides, monstrous and half seen;
of all that rests there, submerged and
opalescent. Deep, deep at the bottom of the sea.
(Desperate. Sings, badly:)
And has suffered a sea-change
into something rich and strange.

(This does not placate anyone.)

FRASER:
And then there's this INSANE dwarf following
me around, following me taking pictures…

(An odd ritual begins:)

(all are locked into the mechanism.)

ALL THREE:
And did the Long white man give you
the coconut?

FRASER:
For the coconut brings good luck; yes, yes,
he did. In sooth.

ALL THREE:
If you have the gift of ivory,
you will be very lucky.

FRASER:
I was not worthy, but I was given
the gift of ivory. Yes, Yes, I was.
In sooth.

—

ALL THREE:
And did the Long White Man make the
fairies dance by moonlight,

DISPUTANT:
Strawberry?

FRASER:
Er,

DISPUTANT:
And? So?

FRASER: *(With great difficulty)*
He said: "I shall teach you how to knead
the white triangular cake of Saint Wolof";
and he did.

ALL THREE:
And he did.

FRASER: He said: "I shall make for you white witches
sensible of the stroke of the white elder at seven miles";
and he did.

ALL THREE:
And he did.

FRASER:
Yes, he did. *(Finally broken)*

(A sudden quiet)

(We hear the snowy wind high above, in the eaves.)

(The three women above BIANCA, JULIA *and* MOTH] *sing a
wordless hymn of thanks.)*

DISPUTANT: *(Quietly)*
So, you do admit.

FRASER:
Yes, it is all true.

DISPUTANT:
All of it?

FRASER:
Yes, allof it.

DISPUTANT:
You admit this all? All of your own free
will?

FRASER:
Er,

DISPUTANT:
All of your own free will? Under no compulsion?

FRASER:
Under no compulsion. Yes.

DISPUTANT:
And you admit you bartered away what is
most precious in an evilish compact
with that certain gentleman…

FRASER:
…at the Ivory Room of the Astor, yes.
But I never received that damned silver-tipped claw,
the claw I was promised, no, all I received in return
was a wooden nickel…

(The worldess hymn ceases.)

(An innocent afterthought)

FRASER:
At the time I imagined there was a great future
in wooden nickels. How was I to know?
Skip it.

DISPUTANT:
And to hide your crimes you confined poor
Great Aunty Dahlia to her treasured chiffonnier;
and banished poor Bianca—with her stutter—
to exile in gay Paree, knowing full well
she was doomed to become, through a sordid
series of transformations, to become a PARROT;

(He is shaken;)
and gave to Cousin Julia, the one you
contemptuously term "The Eraser"…
(He writhes in the grip of remorse;)
…and gave to her, her first seemingly
innocent Kodak Instamatic, knowing
full well what might, given her proclivity
for scratching or rubbing out, what
might be the outcome?

*(He accepts the whitest of white judgements upon his white
soul;)*

(his expiation begins; sobbing, etc.)

FRASER: —

(A slow white out begins.)

ALL THREE:

And what will you say to the White Zebra?
And what will you say to the White Zebra?
And what will you say to the White Zebra?

(Fade to White)

*(The Second Entr'Acte [Hoarfrost]: The Marplot trudges
back to the Big House from his meeting with The Disputant
at the abandoned factory. There, the Marplot encounters
the stuffed ZEBRA from earlier. He looks at the ZEBRA. The
ZEBRA looks at him. Next to the ZEBRA there is an old stone
bench. Slowly the heavy snowfall is covering everything.)*

(Pause)

(Silence)

(Pause)

(He stands for a long time looking looking at the ZEBRA.)

*(He has never seen a Zebra in real life before, and this Zebra
is a mighty fine one.)*

FRASER:
Wow.

ZEBRA: —

(The ZEBRA *is the most beautiful creature The Marplot has
ever seen.)*

*(A joyous and brindled pause, after which The Marplot claps
his hands;)*

FRASER:
Wow.

*(He waddles through the thick snow, and sits down on the
little stone bench, next to the* ZEBRA.*)*

ZEBRA: —

FRASER:
That's okay. That's okay. I understand.
I would like to tell you a story, a true
story from my youth. Owing to an accident
of history and the foolhardiness of youth
I ended up a volunteer with the American
Brigade of the Finnish Army in the Winter
War of 1939. I was wholly innocent, at
the time, of the darker implications
of the project, and we were stationed at
Turku in the Karelian Isthmus…

(The Marplot's story is lost in the story of the winter storm.)

(All fades to whitest opalescence.)

*(Scene [Icicle]: Back in the Big House. The fury of the storm
has abated, and as the scene begins we see, through the
windows, a marvelous sunset.* MOTH, JULIA *and* BIANCA
are snapping the palest of wax beans and LOUISA, *seated
facing her across the room, shells cranberry beans, mirroring
the former. It is a good deal quieter than it ought. The*
WHITE DWARF *is lurking, lurking somewhere unseen.)*

LOUISA:
Will Uncle Fraser be home for supper?

MOTH:
No, Louisa. He will not.

LOUISA:
Why not?
Has he decided to return to his mountain
fastness at White Jaw? on the Yukon?
in the remote crag regions of Northwest
Rhode Island? Has he?

(MOTH *looks at* The Ninny *queerly and stops snapping
beans.)*

(The WHITE DWARF *enters and narrates of the stage
directions which follow.)*

(Something odd happens.)

(The smiling faces of the MUSICIANS *appear in the window;)*

(they unsmile;)

(they disappear.)

MOTH:
Louisa.

JULIA:
Louisa.

BIANCA:
Louisa.

LOUISA:
Er, did I say or do something wrong?

(MOTH *looks away.)*

(MOTH *begins snapping beans.)*

JULIA:
Devil raise a hump upon that damnable Marplot,
that Kaiser Fraser...

BIANCA: *(As a parrot)*
Kaiser Fraser.

LOUISA:
Er,

(An ivory pause)

(Something happens somewhere.)

(Someone does something; only it turns out to be a naughty something;)

(so it must be effaced;)

(so it must be done all over again)

(this something is a thought thing—)

(this something is a thought thing—)

(so it must be done over and over till someone [whoever] has got it right.)

(This happens.)

(This happens, and all the time MOTH remains stiff in her chair snapping beans;

(and The Ninny remains motionless in her chair.)

(She devises an imaginary world in her head;)

(a world of white water and alabaster beaches, glowing under a white star.)

(White water crowfoot and white water lilies abound;)

(this world is called "Whizzbang" and she is happy here. The two MUSICIANS *enter, one playing the violin. The other sings:)*

MUSICIAN:
Poor Louisa, poor Louisa,
why are we doing so poorly?
The bugs and the bats are alive,
bright eyes ablaze in the halls

in the walls of the halls of
    "The White Rose", your home.

LOUISA:
Sorry. I was someplace else. For a moment.

MOTH:
Well, he's had a very serious accident, and he
won't be coming back.

LOUISA:
Won't be coming back? Uncle Fraser?

BIANCA:
No. He won't be coming back.

JULIA:
Not ever.

(The song continues:)

ALL:
The big, blank, bucket-faced moon, oh,
the moon has risen early,
for you, just for you, riding a wire
The moon's high wire,
    just for you, just for you.
For Louisa, poor Louisa.
Louisa Outermost Ring;
It's for you alone we sing,
we sing...
(All stop suddenly.)
(Pause. Silence. Pause)
(All begin again; ghostly quiet.)
Hold on, Hold on,
Poor Louisa,
why are we doing so poorly....

LOUISA:
Because...

MOTH: —

LOUISA:
Why can't he come home again?

MOTH:
Because.

LOUISA:
Because why? Because why not?

JULIA:
Because he did not know how to reply.

LOUISA:
Did not know how to reply to WHAT?

BIANCA:
To the White Zebra of course.

(This simply baffles The Ninny, just as you would expect.)

(She sighs, goes back to her cranberry beans;)

MOTH:
You see, Louisa, he was not able to finish
the story he was telling and that story was the
most telling of all.

LOUISA:
All this is my fault, I suppose, er.

MOTH:
Silly ninny. Confine yourself to the
shelling of cranberry beans, while dear
old Moth confines herself to the
telling of a true tale.
Owing to an accident of history, and the
foolhardiness of youth, Fraser$_2$ ended up
a volunteer with the America Brigade of the
Finish Army in the Winter War of 1939. Young
Fraser was wholly innocent, at the time, of the
darker implication of the project, and was
promptly stationed at Turku, in the Karelian
Isthmus.

Young Fraser, like many in those days, believed
 what he had been told: that the Soviet Union
must be stopped in her aggression against
tiny Finland, a truth as apparent to him as
the fact that Stalingrad had been named for
Lenin.
He and a young colleague, Truesdale, came to
be posted on a low bluff, near the outermost ring
of Turku, with an ancient Maxim gun from the Great
War, seven crates of rusty ammunition, and a firing
radius of 45 degrees. The Finns deposited these
young Americans here thinking the main Russian
thrust would come well to the South. Foolish Finns.
Well.

(As she applies some Gum Arabic to her whitish gums)

*(*LOUISA *once more counts imaginary rabbits as they hop on
her knee.)*

MOTH:
For several hours, the two discussed boyish
things such as Fraser's shocking escape
from the altar at the rehearsal of his
wedding to young Dinah Morgan, a relation
to the great magnate of Hartford—and ever
after a source of embarrassment to the family.
Do you think, do you think, Clyde, for
that was Truesdale's Christian name, that I
did the right thing or was I a cad; or
was I a cad to do the right thing? Or
was I not a cad even though the thing
was not the right thing? Or was the
act both wrong and right and hence
undecidable, and therefore was I not
in fact both a cad and not a cad?
Both P and Not P in the symbolic
logic of Nkosi Whiteman Rudge,

his tutor and of late a
disciple of both Russell
and Wittgenstein.

LOUISA: —

MOTH:
Truesdale, ended the conversation
and incidentally, their friendship
forever, with the rude insult:
Why Fraser, you strike me simply
as a passive aggressive hostile fuck!
As it began to darken and glower;
as it began to darken and glower and to
snow rather heavily.
An uncomfortable few minutes passed
with this reply hanging heavily
in the air.
And all this despite Dinah Morgan's exceptional
pallor.
But just at this moment
Fraser happened to catch sight of something rising
slowly out of the snow, at the far end of the
snowy field. A snowy figure, in fact.
(She adjusts the working of her teeth and gums.)
And then another, and then another, and another.
Slowly arising like squat, appalling snowmen
from the snowfield, each indistinguishable in hue
from the field itself; each figure arising then
slowly, very slowly trudging towards the two lads.
What is that? quipped Fraser. Damned if I know,
responded his fellow;
but
what it was, was the Russian Winter Army, yes,
advancing slowly but inexorably across the
snowy field and through the snowy haze.

Young Fraser watched in astonishment, and
so did young Truesdale.
Slowly trudging across the snowy field
of frightening angles and incalculable
vortices.
At three hundred meters Fraser and Truesdale
opened fire, raking the open field from one side
to the other, rat-a-tat-tat, rat-a-tat-tat;
For a time Fraser would fire and Truesdale
would feed the long belt of cartridges; then
Truesdale would fire and Fraser would feed. Oh,
the advancing snowmen would fall silently
one after another, and be buried in the mounting
drifts of snow. Be buried as more and more
snowmen rose behind them in the white mists
beyond, near the edge of the white wood.
And thus it went for hour upon hour. The little
rat-a-tat-tat, rat-a tat-tat of their Maxim,
and the slowly toppling snowmen, advancing
only to be mowed down, row upon row upon row.
All day this went on: the two young boys slowly
raking their forty-five degrees of angle, filling the
snowy vortices of that nameless place with a
death more breathtakingly beautiful than any
Christmas scene. Time passed even as
Time seemed to stop.
And no more snowmen came. All were dead
And for another few minutes the snow fell
and quietly buried all signs of the…
fateful action…
I am not sure how you would denominate
such an event.

LOUISA: (By now listening closely)
A massacre, I would say.

MOTH:
I was just thinking the same thing, Louisa.
A massacre. Yes, I suppose I would call it that.
(Pause for reflection)
The two young men never spoke of this incident; nor
ever exchanged a word. Ever again. I must go now and
check on poor Great Aunty Dahlia. You too
like Fraser and the rest are new to the secrets
of this house, for Great Aunty Dahlia grows unquiet
unless I apply whitening unguents to the creases
and folds of her indescribable pallor. Even now
I can hear the hinges of her cupboard creaking,
creaking ever so slightly.

(MOTH gets up with her bucket of beans, turns out a light and is gone.)

(LOUISA slowly stands and goes to the window.)

(JULIA and BANCA smile at LOUISA, and go out, gravely.)

(MOTH returns, for one last twist of the knife.)

MOTH:
The white identity, his father Fraser$_3$, used to say
is a burden born of successive false effigies.
A row of object zeroes.

(MOTH disappears, leaving poor LOUISA alone.)

(Something happens somewhere.)

(LOUISA stands and speaks, all without the slightest pause;)

LOUISA:
The sky was gray, like that day in the
Karelian Isthmus, but there was a white
gleam behind, and from where I was
sitting I could look down on the town
of Newport, and it was still and quiet
and white, like a picture.

I remembered that it was on that hill
that Moth (or someone very much like her,
maybe even older and more white) taught
me to play an old game called "Whizzbang"
in which one had to dance, and wind in
and out of a pattern in the grass, and
then when one had danced and turned long
enough the other person asks you questions,
and you can't help answering whether you
want to or not, and whatever you are told
to do you feel you have to do it. This
person said there used to be a lot of games
like that that some people knew of, and
there was one by which people could be
turned into anything you liked and an old
man her great grandmother had seen had known
a girl who had been turned into a large
snake. And there was another very ancient
game of dancing and winding and turning,
by which you can take a person out of
himself and hide him away as long as you
like, and his body went walking about
quite empty without any sense in it.
(Suddenly thoughtful)
This was before we Outermost Rings
discovered, quite accidently, you could
do the same thing by photography.
(Suddenly pensive, in her white way)
But I came to that hill because I had been
talked to by the terrible white Zebra, and
I wanted to think of what had happened
the day before, and of the secrets
of the woods. From the place where I was
sitting I could see beyond the town, into
the opening I had found, the opening in
the field, the opening leading to the

question standing at the beginning of things,
where a little brook had let me into an
unknown country. And I pretended I was
following the brook over again and I went
all the way through into my mind.* And
at last I found the wood, and crept into it
under the bushes, and then in the dusk I saw
something that made me feel as if I were
filled with fire,

(Violin plays the tune from "Whiter than the rest...";)

(Everyone, except for FRASER *troops out for the family
photograph, which is now possible.)*

LOUISA:
as if I wanted to dance and sing and
fly up into the air, because I was
changed and wonderful. But what I saw
was that I had not changed at all,
and had not grown old…

(The jubilant PHOTOGRAPHER *sets up the antique camera.)*

LOUISA:
…And I wondered again and again
how such things could happen and
again how Uncle Fraser's rage against
depiction had so totally backfired
and whether Moth's stories were
really true, because in the day time
in the open air everything seemed
quite different from what it was
at night, when I was quite frightened,
and thought I was to be burned alive.

(The bright magnesium flash of the camera ignites a slow)

(fade to [can it be?] black;)

*(a sort of white blackout [in black-light to emphasize the
terrible pallor of their clothes])*

(in which we hear the entire cast sing:)

ALL:
Description is the Beggar
rolling up the floor
cutting up the carpet
upon which*... *(Etc)*

LOUISA:
A white witch, I hope.
(We see her teeth are quite pointed.)

...the Devil poured
bleach of his depiction.
whirling like a djinn.

Pure depiction beggared
white as sin

White as sin; white as sin;
white as sin;
white as sin.

———

(All begin to whirl their white clothes like monstrous blooms.)

(Slow fade to white)

END OF PLAY